EXTINCT

IN THIS SERIES BY BEN GARROD AND GABRIEL UGUETO

Hallucigenia

Dunkleosteus

Trilobite

Lisowicia

Tyrannosaurus rex

Megalodon

Thylacine

Hainan gibbon

ALSO BY BEN GARROD

The Chimpanzee and Me

Ultimate Dinosaurs series:

Diplodocus

Triceratops

Spinosaurus

Tyrannosaurus rex

Stegosaurus

Velociraptor

Ankylosaurus (June 2023)

Microraptor (September 2023)

EXTINCT

HAINAN GIBBON

Ben Garrod

Illustrated by Gabriel Ugueto

ZEPHYR

An imprint of Head of Zeus

This is a Zephyr book, first published in the UK in 2022
by Head of Zeus Ltd
This paperback edition first published in the UK in 2023
by Head of Zeus Ltd, part of Bloomsbury Publishing Plc

9 7 5 3 1 2 4 6 8

A catalogue record for this book is available from
the British Library.

ISBN (PB): 9781838935481
ISBN (E): 9781838935498

Typesetting and design by Nicky Borowiec

Printed and bound in Serbia by Publikum d.o.o.

Head of Zeus Ltd
5–8 Hardwick Street
London EC1R 4RG

WWW.HEADOFZEUS.COM

'Climate change is the greatest threat to human health in the 21st century.'

The World Health Organisation

CONTENTS

INTRODUCTION

FOR AS LONG as there has been life on Earth, there has been extinction, and in time, all species will go extinct. Every day, we hear more and more tragic stories about more and more species closer to extinction. There are scientists, conservationists, charities, universities, communities and a few good governments fighting to save some of our most treasured species and habitats. But, and there is a *but* to this story, extinction has its place in our world and, at the right level and at the right time, it is a perfectly natural occurrence and can even help evolution in some ways.

I am a scientist. It's the best job in the world. In my work, I look at evolution and I've been lucky enough to spend time with some of the most endangered species on our planet, as well as some that have already gone extinct.

I'm fascinated by the effects extinction has on nature. But how much do we *really* know about extinction?

If we are to stand a chance of saving species from extinction, then first we need to understand extinction itself. What is extinction? What causes it? What happens when many species go extinct at once? I want to explore extinction as a biological process and investigate why it can sometimes be a positive thing for evolution, as well as nature's most destructive force. Let's put it under the microscope and find out everything there is to know.

When a species is declared extinct, we place a dagger symbol (†) next to its name when it's listed or mentioned in a scientific manner. So, if you do see the name of a species with a little dagger after it, you'll know why. It's extinct. In this series, I have written about eight fantastic species. Starting with *Hallucigenia* (†), then *Dunkleosteus* (†) trilobites (†), *Lisowicia* (†), *Tyrannosaurus rex* (†) and megalodon (†), before finishing with thylacine (†) and lastly, the Hainan gibbon. Of these, only the Hainan gibbon does not have a dagger next to its scientific name, meaning it is an animal we still have a chance of saving from extinction.

The eagle-eyed among you will notice I've approached this book slightly differently from the other titles in the series. I've asked four experts – a psychologist, a marine ecologist, an earth scientist and a primatologist – to share their knowledge with us. My questions are: Is nature good? Why are marine environments so important? Hasn't our climate always changed? And, what's it like to work with some of the rarest apes in the world? In this book I've swapped the order of the chapters to write about the animal first and then the mass extinction event. Because that's where you come in!

Ready? Let's fit another piece into the jigsaw puzzle of the story of life on Earth.

Professor Ben Garrod

WHAT IS EXTINCTION?

OFTEN, IN BIOLOGY, as is the case with much of science, there are complicated definitions for complicated terms. Understanding the essence of extinction, though, is not especially complicated – it is when the species is dead. Not just the individual animal or a large group of animals which are the same, but all animals of that species. When the last one dies and there are no more left alive, that species is extinct. Lost. Gone forever.

Something I have trouble with when we talk about extinction is the question, 'So what? Who really cares if a species dies out? What difference does it really make?

So what if another type of frog disappears?' The truth is there are people who will never be convinced that it's vitally important we fight against extinction. They're frequently the same people who don't believe our climate is rapidly changing, and who argue against much of modern science.

So why *does* it matter if a species disappears? There's a simple answer and a more complicated answer. The simple answer is that as humans, we occupy a unique position in the animal kingdom. We understand a great deal. We have the power and the ability to completely shape and control the world around us, and that comes with a duty to protect others within our community, whether they're our human neighbours or our animal neighbours in forests and reefs and in our gardens.

The second answer to the question is that the natural world is a wondrous interconnected ecosystem, in which species link to one another.

Nature is like a big spider web, connecting billions of organisms with invisible threads. If one species is removed, it pulls on another part of that web. And if enough species are made extinct, then the whole structure is destroyed. There are many species of plants, animals, fungi and other life, and it's hard to know what catastrophic effect a species going extinct might lead to.

For example, sharks, tuna and turtles all prey on jellyfish. If these predators are removed from an ocean ecosystem, jellyfish numbers then shoot up and suddenly there are so many that they are doing much better than small fish like sardines. The jellyfish eat so much plankton that food chains collapse and the dangerous species of jellyfish can make beaches unsafe places for us.

Because of the balance within this global web of life, killing sharks can make swimming in the sea more dangerous.

Extinction has been present since the first life on Earth popped into existence, which must mean that loads *and loads* of species have gone extinct. It's hard to get your head around how many. Scientists predict that 99 per cent of all the species that have *ever* lived have gone extinct. And if you're wondering just how many species that might actually be, then if their calculations are correct, it means we have already lost an almost unbelievable five billion species from our planet.

We cannot be certain because many of the extinctions stretch back millions (or even hundreds of millions) of years and, because there wasn't a scientist there with a camera or notebook, we shall never know about many of these losses. Scientists believe that there may be 10–14

Woolly mammoth

Dodo

million different species (although some believe this figure might be as high as one trillion) but of those, only 1.2 million have been documented and recorded in a proper scientific way. This means we don't know about 90 per cent of life on planet Earth right now.

Here's where it gets a little complicated. Extinction is natural. Even human beings will go extinct one day. It might sound sad but that's because you're thinking from the point of view of a person. We are simply one of those 14 million or so species, remember. Usually, a species has about 10 million years or so of evolving, eating, chasing, playing, maybe doing homework, building nests or even going to the moon before it goes extinct and ends up in the history (or even prehistory) books. Some last longer than this, some are around for less time.

Eurasian lynx

ASK THE EXPERT

Professor Richard Pancost is Head of the School of Earth Sciences at the University of Bristol, Professor of Biogeochemistry and a member of the Cabot Institute for the Environment. He researches how organisms mediate our planet's chemical environment, and he uses their molecular fossils to reconstruct Earth's past climate. He is particularly interested in exploring past Earth system responses to rapid global warming and the sustainability of ecosystems on which we depend.

Hasn't our climate always changed?

It has; and the same methods that help us understand how climate has changed help us understand why it has changed.

Earth's climate has been globally stable for about the past 10,000 years, but even so, parts of the Earth have experienced regionally dramatic change, from the Little Ice Age in Europe to a prolonged north African Humid period that ended about 6,000 years ago.

Further back into time, the changes are much larger and more global, including the fluctuating glacial and interglacial cycles of the Pleistocene, in which massive ice sheets expanded over much of Europe, Asia and North America and then retreated, again and again. Each time, they left evidence of their invasion, with terminal glacial deposits, scoured rocks and geochemical signals in the deep ocean.

Even further back, forests in the Arctic Circle and on the shoreline of ancient Antarctica speak of a world far warmer than today, an interpretation supported not just by many other fossils (including Arctic crocodiles and palms) and a lack of glacial deposits but also by a rich variety of specific, tell-tale chemical traces. And so it goes, throughout the history of the Earth: the greenhouse climates of the Cretaceous and the Eocene; the rapid global warming at the Permo-Triassic Boundary 252 million years ago, which we link to the Great Dying mass extinction; and even the 'Snowball Earth' of the Cryogenian (over 650 million years ago).

When we take a look at those same tell-tale chemical traces, whether they're geochemical (the processes behind the formation of the Earth's major geological features such as oceans and even the Earth's crust), or in the form of sediment or even fossils, they also reveal the drivers of Earth's climate change – Earth's relationship with the sun, plate tectonics and greenhouse gases. Swings in Earth's orbit cause summer sunlight to fall differently on the Northern

Hemisphere, pacing those glacial–interglacial cycles. The long-term drifting of the continents can open and close ocean gateways, changing ocean currents and therefore the climate of entire continents.

And carbon dioxide concentrations drive both slow and rapid climate change. Over millions of years, the rebalancing of carbon release via volcanism or burial in ocean sediments shaped extended intervals of greenhouse or icehouse Earth. In some instances, perhaps due to the intrusion of magma into organic-rich rocks, carbon dioxide was released rapidly and caused dramatic but transient warming. And so, just as we know that carbon dioxide caused the Earth to warm in the past, its sudden release today due to the burning of fossil fuels has caused Earth to warm and will cause it to continue to do so.

However, the current rate of carbon dioxide transfer from ancient sediments into the Earth's atmosphere is far faster than those ancient 'geologically rapid' CO_2 release events – it is a rate of change nearly without precedent in Earth's history and its consequences on life could be dramatic.

WHY DO SPECIES GO EXTINCT?

A SPECIES doesn't know it's going extinct. There's no sense of getting lonelier and lonelier among the last remaining Galápagos tortoises, or the few vaquita, spoon-billed sandpipers or Chinese giant salamanders left. Only our own species has that ability.

If they did know extinction was coming, what do you think different species would do? Learn to run faster, move to higher ground to avoid flooding, start eating different food? They might try to prepare for the changes ahead of them to avoid the approaching devastation. Sadly, nature isn't like that and wildlife doesn't consciously prepare for changes ahead. But in a weird way, on some level, *something* like this does happen.

As temperatures slowly rise, species evolve to tolerate the increases, or they move to a different part of their habitat or environment, where the temperature is less extreme. If an aquatic environment becomes more acidic or less oxygenated, then maybe organisms can evolve to manage such environmental changes. If organisms are given enough time to adapt, or are physically able to respond to the changes around them, they stand a chance of survival. But if changes occur too quickly, or are too severe, then species are less likely to adapt and more likely to die. In the worst-case scenario, the entire species dies and goes extinct.

There are almost limitless reasons which can lead to extinction but they have one thing in common. They all focus on change. These changes can be either in the species' 'physical environment', such as the destruction of a habitat, through flooding or drought. The change might be in its 'biological environment', such as the arrival of a new predator, or the development of a new deadly disease.

There are a variety of general causes that can lead, directly or indirectly, to the extinction of a species or group of species:

DISEASES, PREDATION AND COMPETITION

Diseases are often linked to extinction. Practically every species alive has its own set of diseases and those which it can pick up from other species. One group of diseases which are linked to extinctions are the zoonotic (ZOO not-ik) diseases. They originate in animals other than humans, but can spread to humans. Some of the worst, and most common, diseases we know are zoonotic. Everything from Ebola and COVID-19, to leprosy, rabies and even the plague are zoonotic. These diseases are obviously a major problem for us and cause untold pain and suffering, but some can also be passed back into animals, where they rip through either wild or captive populations.

The COVID-19 virus, which is responsible for the most recent pandemic affecting our own species, arrived from an animal species we haven't yet been able to identify. What is interesting, though, is that the same virus also affects mink, a species related to weasels and badgers. In Denmark, where mink is 'farmed' in huge numbers, killed and used for 'luxury' (and disgusting) fur coats, 15 million mink were destroyed after some of them contracted the virus. Similarly, Ebola is able to infect wild great apes, such as chimpanzees and gorillas, making zoonotic diseases a significant risk in terms of an extinction threat.

When we think of predators, it's easy to picture lions, polar bears, sharks, eagles and crocodiles, but there is a species that hunts and kills all other species, and I'm sorry to say there are no prizes for guessing which species that is.

We not only kill every other species out there, other predators included, but we exploit them in ways that no other predators do. In a traditional sense, we act as predators when we hunt animals for food. Among the worst examples of this is sharks being killed for their fins. Although there's little meat on a fin and no taste, they're used to make shark fin soup, which sells in many Asian countries for hundreds of pounds or dollars. Over 100 million sharks are killed every year, just for this expensive, tasteless soup, made to look fancy and impress your friends.

We exploit animals in other ways too. We hunt them for their skins, their tusks and their feathers and even trap them to make them our pets. Monkeys, for example, which never make good pets, are kept in many countries. In the UK, around 5,000 monkeys and lemurs are living like this, which drives their extinction in the wild.

Life is tough enough for any species, as they deal with predators, harsh environments and the daily struggle for survival. It gets worse when they have to compete with other species for food or somewhere to live. Competition is either natural, such as with leopards, lions and hyenas competing for food on the savannas of East Africa or, caused by humans – for instance, overfishing in the oceans means less food for sharks.

Competition is natural in every species, whether it's an oak sapling competing with other tree species in a forest, or a small reef fish trying to find food alongside hundreds of others, but there comes a point when competition is too much. If we placed all the mammals alive today in a big pile, then separated them into three smaller heaps, you could see the stress wild mammals are under.

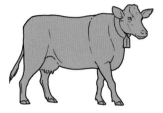

One of these piles of mammals, humans, would represent 34 per cent of the total weight (we call this biomass). The biggest heap would be farmed mammals (or livestock), such as cows, sheep and pigs, which would account for 62 per cent of the total. If you're quick at maths, you'll already know that the remaining heap is pretty small, and that wild mammals would be just 4 per cent of the world's total biomass for mammals. Humans and farmed animals aren't directly competing with wild animals in the way two different shark species or two different bats might, but they still need food, water, space, and it is this that is driving many species into extinction.

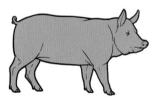

COEXTINCTION

Sometimes, a species has evolved alongside another species so closely that when one goes extinct, there is nothing the other can do but go extinct too. This might be a specific parasite depending on a specific host, or a particular pollinating insect needing a species of plant in order to survive. An example of coextinction is the decline of a species of red ant in southern England, which, in 1979, resulted in the local extinction of the large blue butterfly. The butterfly caterpillar lives inside the ants' nest, where it eats ant larvae, or begs for food from the adult ants. Without the ants, the butterfly slipped into extinction. Now, after lots of conservation work, including habitat restoration for the ants, large blue butterflies have been reintroduced and are found across 33 sites in the southwest of England. A very welcome conservation story with a happy ending.

The natural world is delicately connected, so the existence of some species depends on others. Sometimes the loss of one species may lead to the extinction of another. The caterpillar of the large blue butterfly lives in the nests of red ants and tricks the ants into feeding it. The butterfly species needs the ants in order to survive.

GENETIC MIXING

Every species has its own set of unique genetic data. It's like the species' recipe. If a little bit of it is changed, then it's a different species. Likewise, some species are more closely related to one another than to others. Closely related species sometimes breed and produce what we call hybrids. When this happens, there is a risk that one (or even both) of the original species could eventually go extinct, with the combined mixture of their offspring taking over. There is nothing wrong with this, but it does change that original species 'recipe'.

HABITAT DESTRUCTION

When we talk about this cause of extinction, we often use the phrase 'habitat loss' but, to be blunt, we don't *lose* habitats, we *destroy* them. Admitting what we actually do is a big step in the right direction needed to protect habitats and ecosystems around the world. The saddest thing about

habitat destruction is that it means devastation, not only for many individual organisms, but also sometimes for entire species.

Increasing food production is a major agent for the conversion of natural habitat into agricultural land across terrestrial environments, but habitat destruction also has a devastating impact on marine environments. We have recently seen the first modern-day marine fish extinction. The smooth handfish was among 13 species of bizarre-looking fish that could 'walk' on its fins. Only one museum specimen exists and none have been seen in the wild for around 200 years. Driven by damaging fishing techniques and habitat destruction, the species was confirmed as being extinct in 2020.

Habitat destruction is a leading factor associated with species extinction and is identified as a main threat to 85 per cent of all species that are described as being either 'Threatened', 'Endangered' or 'Critically Endangered'.

CLIMATE CHANGE

This has been a major factor in every previous mass extinction in some way, shape or form. Climate changes all the time in cycles, enabling us to look back and assess how these changes occur and by how much the climate changes. Although the climate across the globe is currently changing, through increased rain and flooding in some areas and increased droughts and fires in others, temperature increases are a good way to establish how things are changing.

I looked at temperatures across the planet today, as I was writing, to make sure my content is as accurate and as recent as possible, and what I discovered shocked me. Last week, forest fires raged across Canada, as temperatures there reached a scorching 49.6°C. Similar temperatures, of around 48°C, have been experienced in Siberia in Russia, in a heatwave that has lasted for weeks. These temperatures in Canada and Russia both fall within the

Arctic Circle, an area known for its fragile cold habitats. Although the Arctic is rapidly heating, the story is the same for the southern pole. Last year, Antarctica observed a new record high temperature of 18.3°C, which is responsible for the rapid loss of sea ice.

Today saw a new record set. In Death Valley in North America, the temperature reached 54.4°C, and although Death Valley is well known for being a hot and inhospitable place, this is the highest reliably recorded temperature ever anywhere on the planet. Climate change is a big factor for previous mass extinctions, and we'll talk about it later in the book. Not because there isn't much to say, but because there's *so much* to say regarding climate change and the mass extinction we're facing.

All around the planet, the climate, as well as weather, is changing and there are more storms, floods, droughts and fires. This koala is lucky to escape a huge bushfire burning across the Australian outback.

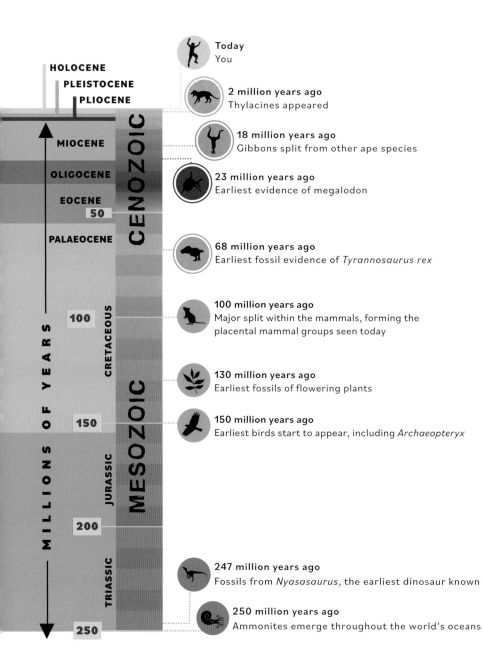

HOLOCENE
PLEISTOCENE
PLIOCENE

CENOZOIC

MIOCENE

OLIGOCENE

EOCENE
50

PALAEOCENE

MILLIONS OF YEARS

100

CRETACEOUS

MESOZOIC

150

JURASSIC

200

TRIASSIC

250

Today
You

2 million years ago
Thylacines appeared

18 million years ago
Gibbons split from other ape species

23 million years ago
Earliest evidence of megalodon

68 million years ago
Earliest fossil evidence of *Tyrannosaurus rex*

100 million years ago
Major split within the mammals, forming the placental mammal groups seen today

130 million years ago
Earliest fossils of flowering plants

150 million years ago
Earliest birds start to appear, including *Archaeopteryx*

247 million years ago
Fossils from *Nyasasaurus*, the earliest dinosaur known

250 million years ago
Ammonites emerge throughout the world's oceans

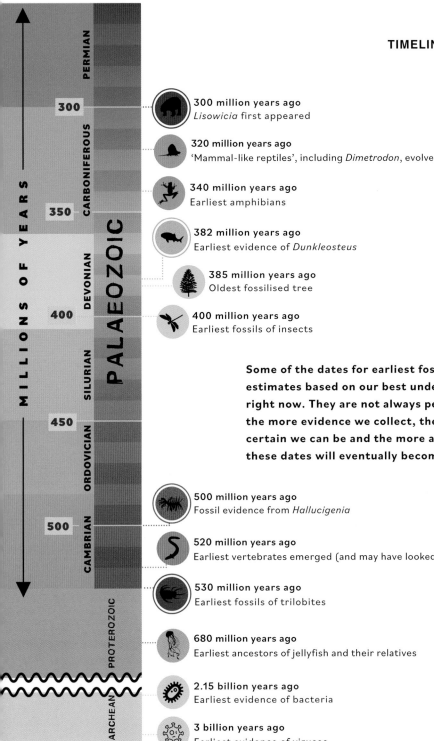

MILLIONS OF YEARS

PALAEOZOIC

PERMIAN

300

CARBONIFEROUS

350

DEVONIAN

400

SILURIAN

450

ORDOVICIAN

CAMBRIAN

500

PROTEROZOIC

ARCHEAN

300 million years ago
Lisowicia first appeared

320 million years ago
'Mammal-like reptiles', including *Dimetrodon*, evolve

340 million years ago
Earliest amphibians

382 million years ago
Earliest evidence of *Dunkleosteus*

385 million years ago
Oldest fossilised tree

400 million years ago
Earliest fossils of insects

Some of the dates for earliest fossils are estimates based on our best understanding right now. They are not always perfect and the more evidence we collect, the more certain we can be and the more accurate these dates will eventually become.

500 million years ago
Fossil evidence from *Hallucigenia*

520 million years ago
Earliest vertebrates emerged (and may have looked like small eels)

530 million years ago
Earliest fossils of trilobites

680 million years ago
Earliest ancestors of jellyfish and their relatives

2.15 billion years ago
Earliest evidence of bacteria

3 billion years ago
Earliest evidence of viruses

MASS EXTINCTIONS

RIGHT NOW, somewhere in the world, something will be going extinct, hopefully due to natural causes. In the same way that the evolution and appearance of a species is completely natural, so too is the constant loss of species. They come and go, a bit like tides moving back and forth, or the changing of the seasons.

Extinction is unavoidable and goes on at a fairly predictable rate wherever life exists. We call this background extinction: constant, low-level extinction which doesn't cause major problems on a wider scale, other than for the species going extinct, that is. These 'everyday extinctions' go mostly unnoticed by the majority of us. This all changes when we talk about a mass extinction.

For the purposes of my books, we are going to treat a mass extinction as the worldwide loss of about 75 per cent (or more) of species, over a short space of 'geological' time. If you're wondering how short 'a short space of geological time' is, then let's say it has to be under three million years. This might sound a very long time, but remember Earth is around four and a half *billion* years old. By making our timeframe three million years we catch the sudden disastrous mass extinctions, such as the dinosaur-killing asteroid End Cretaceous event, as well as some of the mass extinctions which played out over hundreds of thousands, or even millions, of years ago.

Mass extinctions, as you might expect, involve loss of life on an enormous scale, either across a large number of species or groups, or across a significant part of the planet, or both. In a mass extinction event, the rate of species being lost is greater than the rate by which species are evolving – imagine you're slowly filling a bucket with water, but there's a big hole in its side; over time, the bucket will still become empty. Over the last 500 million years or so, the Earth has experienced multiple mass extinctions, ranging from five to as many as 20 depending on the definitions (and there are a number of different ones) scientists use. In the worst of these mass extinction events, over 90 per cent of life on Earth was wiped out, and in terms of life recovering, it may take at least 10 million years for biodiversity levels to return to what they were.

When we talk about mass extinctions, most scientists agree that there have been five classic mass extinctions, with the earliest occurring around 450 million years ago and the most recent about 66 million years ago. In addition to these famous five mass extinctions, another has been identified recently, which struck around 2.5 million years ago.

Many scientists say we are entering (or even in) the sixth mass extinction event, but this is something that needs to be looked at closely for two reasons. First, I've just mentioned the recently identified mass extinction which occurred around 2.5 million years ago, which would make that the sixth mass extinction and the current global extinction event the seventh. Second, it's really hard to say exactly when most mass extinctions start, so, as bad as it is right now, we may not even be in one yet.

Throughout the series, we look at the five classic mass extinctions, a newly discovered mass extinction and the current extinction event, which is being triggered by us. Finally, in this book, we take a deeper look at what's happening across the planet now, how scientists and conservationists are tackling the threat of extinction and exploring what can be done.

Professor Gillian Forrester is an evolutionary psychologist at Birkbeck, University of London. She explores who humans are and how we are connected to the natural world. She studies the similarities and differences between the brains and the behaviours of humans, chimpanzees, gorillas and orangutans, and she is a conservationist.

Is nature good?

It is easy to forget that we are animals and that we share this planet with millions of other living things, coexisting as part of a global ecosystem with a delicate balance. By treating ourselves as separate from other plants and animals, we can upset the natural balance of our planet.

When we focus entirely on our own needs, without taking into consideration just how our behaviours impact other species around us, we can cause serious damage.

For example, when we cut down forests for building materials, mine the earth for minerals or clear land for farming, we use up important resources and habitats that are needed for other plants and animals to thrive. This causes some species to lose their food sources or their homes, or both, which may eventually result in that plant or animal dying out completely.

This is a problem not only for the affected species, but also for the physical wellbeing of humans. We are part of the Earth's natural systems and we rely upon rich biodiversity to survive. Healthy ecosystems produce the natural things we need to live: the fresh water we drink, the clean air we breathe and the healthy plants and animals we consume.

Our connection with the natural world also has an effect on our mental wellbeing. Concerns about how we use the world's resources and the damage we cause to other species is leading many people to suffer from stress and anxiety – so much so that 'eco-anxiety' has become a problem of its own.

However, learning about our connection to other animals can not only help us to understand the world around us, but also make us more compassionate. It makes us care more about the plants and animals around us, which can significantly improve our mental wellbeing.

Spending time in green spaces, like parks and forests, is linked to people being happier, even after they have gone home. Getting involved in positive conservation activities can also have a positive effect on mental wellbeing. You don't have to go further than your own back garden or a park nearby to connect with nature. Learn about your native wildlife, help out with local bird and insect surveys, or plant some butterfly- and bee-friendly flowers. Small actions by individuals make a huge difference.

HAINAN GIBBON

THE HAINAN (HI-nan) gibbon is famous for all the wrong reasons. It is the world's rarest gibbon, the rarest ape, rarest primate, and quite possibly the rarest species of mammal on the planet. In the middle of the 20th century, there were around 2,000 Hainan gibbons living across the island of Hainan, which sits off the southern coast of China. Over the next 50 years or so, their numbers crashed, with barely any surviving as we entered the 21st century. Now, fewer than 35 individuals remain in the wild, while there are none in captivity in zoos or sanctuaries.

When scientists assess how common or how rare a species is, they place it in one of several categories. Some, such as 'Least Concern' are not a problem for conservationists, whereas others, such as 'Vulnerable' are in moderate trouble. 'Endangered' means they are facing a serious threat. The Hainan gibbon is in a category called 'Critically Endangered', which is worse than being endangered and is a step away from being extinct.

DISCOVERY

For many species which have either gone extinct or are sitting close to the edge of extinction, there are rarely detailed records of what life was like before they died out. We have no records for *Tyrannosaurus rex*, *Dunkleosteus* or megalodon from before they died, as each went extinct millions of years before our own species arrived on the planet.

But we do have records for the Hainan gibbon. They show that the species was once found not only all over the island of Hainan but also across nearly half of China, according to some government records dating from the 17th century. Some may not have been the same species, though, because the geography of this area would have created river, valley and mountain barriers, allowing for more than one species. Because records from then weren't detailed, and without either photography or DNA techniques, we can't be sure these historical records were for the same species.

After a significant drop in population, specifically between the 1950s and 1980s, a report from the early 2000s found just 15 gibbons were left, in two small family groups and two lone individuals. A year later, the maximum population size (and the global total) was just 19 gibbons. All these animals were found in an area called the Bawangling (ba-wang ling) National Nature Reserve.

ANATOMY

I've not seen Hainan gibbons in the wild, but I have been lucky enough to see a few different gibbon species when I worked in Indonesia and they always look like something between a trapeze artist and a teddy bear on a rocket as they move through their forest homes. Their long arms and lightweight bodies allow them to swing through the canopy, and they have a range of extra adaptations which help them be skilled aerial acrobats.

An adult Hainan gibbon weighs 6–8kg, which is about the same weight as either a King Charles spaniel or a microwave oven in your home. The gibbon is, however, much more agile than both a small, friendly dog or a microwave oven! It has a little crown-like tuft of dark hair on the top of its head, which gives it its other name of Hainan black-crested gibbon.

We see something known as sexual dichromatism (DI-cro-ma tiz-um) in Hainan gibbons, which means the male and female are different colours. The adult male is black, while an adult female is light yellow or orange-yellow with a dark patch on her head, and becomes grey-brown with age. Newborn Hainan gibbons are light yellow, similar in colour to an adult female, but after about a month, they begin to darken and become completely black by about three months old, similar in colour to the adult male. When a female becomes mature, between five and eight years of age, her hair colour changes to light yellow or orange-yellow. A male does not change colour and remains black throughout its life.

The most obvious features in any gibbon species are its long arms and legs. A gibbon uses its long, powerful arms to swing through the trees, using a repeated motion of swing after swing after swing. This is a specialised method of movement called brachiation (BRAY-KEY AY-shun) and is only seen in gibbons.

High up in the forest canopy, a mother Hainan gibbon sits with her baby, as the darker male surveys their territory.

Brachiation accounts for as much as 80 per cent of movement in some species of gibbon. Between letting go of one branch and before grabbing the next, a Hainan gibbon is able to sail through the air for as much as 12m, the same as about 12 large adult steps (a lot further than you can jump, I'm guessing). When brachiating, it is able to move as fast as 55km per hour. It can make individual leaps of up to 8m and can walk on its hind legs, balancing with its arms raised in the air. Gibbons are the fastest and most agile of all tree-dwelling, non-flying mammals. Other types of primate which swing don't fully use brachiation.

I usually get you to try some experiments, but I won't suggest you try to brachiate. Partly because I'd worry you'd hurt yourself, moving through a forest canopy faster than a speeding car, but also because I know you can't brachiate, however hard you try! That's because in order to brachiate, you need a special adaptation in your wrists. You have different types of joints, which connect bones to one another and allow different types of movement. Joints, such as ball and socket joints, in your shoulder and your hip, allow movement in different directions, and hinge joints, such as those in your elbow and knee, only open and close in one direction. Your wrist joint is an example of what's called a gliding joint. Movement is limited and is based on smooth surfaces sliding over one another. The wrist joint of a gibbon (including the Hainan gibbon) looks and acts more like a ball and socket joint, with part of the joint rounded and sitting inside the cup-like structure of the other part of the joint. This allows a much larger range of movement, and reduces the amount of energy needed in the upper arm and body.

Siamang

Western hoolock gibbon

Bornean white-bearded gibbon

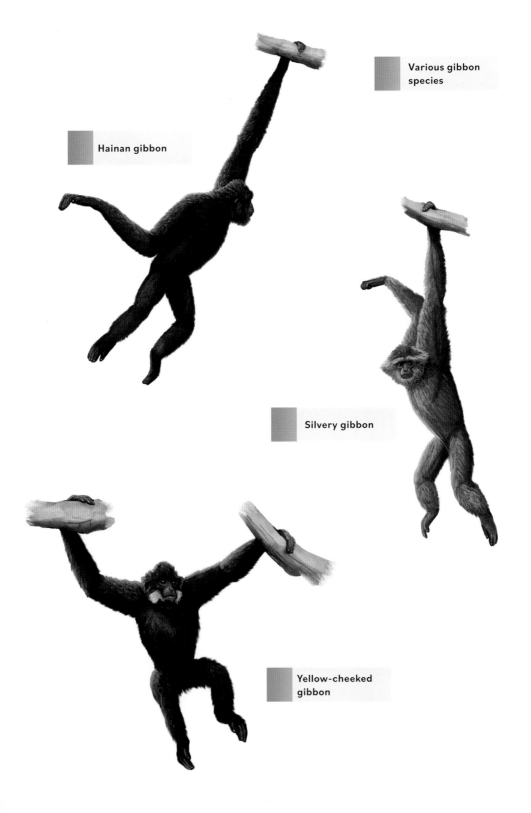

Various gibbon species

Hainan gibbon

Silvery gibbon

Yellow-cheeked gibbon

CLASSIFICATION

If we look further back to see when gibbons appeared in the fossil record, the group to which Hainan gibbons belong appears in the record in the Early Pleistocene period, around three million years ago. Although the record is patchy, we can trace gibbons back to see when the group first appeared after splitting away from their nearest relatives. They are part of the ape community, which includes humans, chimpanzees, bonobos, gorillas, orangutans and gibbons, but the gibbons became a separate group when they split off and evolved their own unique traits between 20 and 16 million years ago. Although some species of gibbons have gone extinct, we currently recognise 18 different species, which sit in four groups.

There has been confusion and disagreement over the classification of gibbons for many years. They're a complex group to separate and understand, and conservationists have used genetics, anatomy and even their song to help identify and classify the different species.

For much of the 20th century, the Hainan gibbon was thought to be the same as the black-crested gibbon found in mainland China. Other scientists thought it was a little bit different, but not enough to be a separate species, so the Hainan was said to be a subspecies of the black-crested gibbon. Later, it was thought to be the same as the critically endangered Cao-vit gibbon, found in a small area on the border between China and Vietnam. When DNA analysis was carried out, scientists were able to be more certain of how they should classify the Hainan gibbon. Along with differences in its coat colour and distinct calls, the genetic results helped show it is a completely separate species. As well as being its own species, the Hainan gibbon represents a very old split within the gibbon family tree, separating about three million years ago from the other gibbon species alive today.

As with so many other areas of biology, and science in general, this shows just how much science is like a detective story, full of twists and turns and clues, but also how important it is to keep on collecting data and doing the research, in order to fully understand the topic. The more we know, the more we understand.

ECOLOGY AND ENVIRONMENT 🌍

Gibbons live in tropical and subtropical rainforest from eastern Bangladesh to northeast India and from Malaysia, Thailand and Vietnam to southern China and Indonesia, including the islands of Sumatra, Borneo and Java.

The climate across Hainan is hot and humid and the forest sits on steep slopes within valleys and ravines. The climate is dominated by tropical monsoons, which see large shifts in weather patterns, going from dry seasons to very wet seasons, brought about by strong winds. In January and February, temperatures are around 16°C, although this increases to 29°C in the summer months, even to as high as 35°C. In some of the mountainous areas, the temperature can drop much lower in the winter months.

When the rains come, there's a lot of it, up to 2.4m a year in the area where the gibbons live. The Hainan gibbon is now only found in mountainous rainforest, 800–1100m above sea level. The remaining gibbons spend nearly all their time in the trees, where they feed on a range of leaves and fruits.

Researchers have estimated that the gibbons eat at least 100 different species of plants within their forest home.

We don't really think of wild animals as having jobs, but gibbons have an important role to play within their natural habitats, and the Hainan gibbon is no exception. It helps distribute seeds around the forest, planting them with a little dollop of fertiliser. If you're puzzled by this, then think about it. They eat a lot of fruit. Lots of the fruit contains seeds, which aren't digested. They have to come out somewhere, and when they do, they come out in a bit of poo which will help them grow. It may sound gross, but this is very important for keeping forests rich in biodiversity.

Although the danger of predation is rare for the Hainan gibbon, if we ignore the threat posed by humans, they would naturally be hunted by clouded leopards, black bears, pythons and large birds of prey.

The Hainan gibbon lives in three different types of forest habitats across the island. The first (and best) is the primary forest, which is mature, old-growth forest. Within this habitat, the gibbon is usually found in trees at least 10m in height. Much of this primary forest habitat was destroyed during the 20th century by logging activity and for rubber plantations, leaving only 4 per cent of the original habitat. Over 25 per cent of the Hainan gibbon's habitat has been destroyed due to illegal pulp paper plantations. As their habitat has reduced more and more, the gibbon has been driven into less suitable habitats at higher altitudes, in mountainous regions.

The gibbon also inhabits secondary forest, which is forest that has been logged to some level, but has started to regrow, with a big mix of new trees among the more mature parts of the forest. Secondary forest habitats have more, but shorter, trees and fewer resources such as food and water. This habitat isn't as good for a population of healthy gibbons.

The dwarf forests are even worse and, given the opportunity, the Hainan gibbon spends less than 1 per cent of its time there. Constant habitat destruction, however, is forcing the Hainan gibbon to spend more time in less favourable habitats.

Where

Hainan is 32,900 square
kilometres in size and
sits off the southern coast of
mainland China. The island is
classed as a mixture of subtropical and
tropical habitats. The last remaining Hainan
gibbons live in a 300 square kilometre protected area in
the west of the island, called the Bawangling National
Nature Reserve.

When

From the best evidence we have, the group to which the
Hainan gibbon belongs emerged in the Early Pleistocene
across China, around three million years ago. Although
their numbers have dropped massively, they are still alive,
sadly in very low numbers.

BEHAVIOUR

The Hainan gibbon is a social animal, a characteristic shared by all other gibbons and, to a greater or lesser extent, by all other primates.

It is fiercely territorial, but unlike many territorial animals it chooses not to fight but instead display to one another and *sing* to its competitors. The vocal display can be heard from up to a kilometre away and is formed by a two-part song between a male and female. If there are any young animals in the group, they may also join in with the calling. Each gibbon species has a unique song, which helps identify them, but scientists are also able to use these calls to help locate different family groups within a forest habitat. Hainan gibbons also sing their duets for mating and bonding between couples.

The song starts in the early morning, with periods of singing lasting for five to 20 minutes. Early morning songs help reinforce the bond between a male and female, as well as warning any other gibbons within earshot that this is *their* territory.

A gibbon family group, which consists of one adult male and up to two adult females, defends a territory typically around 1.49 square kilometres in size. Each female gives birth to a single offspring every two years. If there are two females in the same family, they alternate the births, resulting in one newborn a year for the family group.

Baby Hainan gibbons remain almost constantly attached to their mothers for the first eight or nine months of their lives. When they reach about two years old, they can move about on their own to explore, feed and play, and they eventually leave their family group when they reach maturity, at between five and eight years old, so they can join another family, or start their own family. Gibbon males and females often pair for life.

Dr Carolyn Thompson is a Swiss-British primatologist (a scientist who studies primates: monkeys, apes, lemurs and tarsiers). She has 15 years' experience in this field, eight of which have been focused on gibbons. She is currently a PhD researcher at University College London and the Zoological Society of London's Institute of Zoology. In her spare time, Carolyn writes primate-themed children's books for conservation organisations.

What is it like to work with some of the rarest apes on the planet?

Have you ever heard an ape sing? Or seen one clear a 12m distance in a single swing? Your first gibbon encounter is unforgettable; ironic, given that they are referred to as the 'forgotten' apes (receiving less funding and research attention compared to their great ape cousins).

You wake up when it's still dark and force yourself out of bed. You throw on some old clothes before grabbing your backpack which contains everything you need for your day's work: first aid kit, compass, water, lunch and your datasheets. You set off from your base camp into the forest, using your head torch to guide you. As dawn emerges, the forest sings itself to life. Over orchestral bird calls and screeching cicadas, you hear the most

haunting and beautiful song. The song of the gibbons.

My first encounter with gibbons was in Indonesian Borneo while I was working for a conservation organisation. I was shocked to learn that 19 of the 20 species were on the brink of extinction, due to disappearing habitats, hunting and trade. Hearing the gibbons sing, I knew I had found my song too.

I now work with three of the rarest gibbons found in isolated forest fragments in China and Vietnam. These include the world's rarest primate, the Hainan gibbon, with fewer than 35 individuals remaining.

Work with wild gibbons involves following these agile apes as they fly through the trees. I frantically try and record where they are going, what they are feeding on, and who they are socialising with. But not all my work is in the forest. To investigate why we are losing gibbons so quickly, we need to understand human–gibbon interactions.

As most gibbon conservation issues are caused by people, it makes sense to involve people in the solution.

I have the privilege of immersing myself in local community life to understand people's values and attitudes towards the gibbons, with the aim of developing strategies for sustainable coexistence. I often find myself helping with coffee farming, joining traditional dances with my two left feet, and partaking in culinary adventures sampling duck brain and the 100-year-old egg. (This is a Chinese delicacy in which eggs are fermented in strong black tea, lime, salt and freshly burnt wood ash, then left for two to five months, not a century as the name suggests!)

Fieldwork with gibbons is always unexpected. And although it is sometimes challenging and harrowing, it is an honour to work tirelessly for the rarest apes, whose singing can still be heard despite their dwindling numbers. Their song, to me, serves as a loud and important reminder that they are still here.

THE ANTHROPOCENE MASS EXTINCTION

THE LIST OF mass extinction events isn't a long one, but it is still a list that has changed the face of our planet multiple times. Each mass extinction has been unique, either in the way it was caused or in the effects it had. However, none of the previous mass extinctions has been caused by a single species. Until now. There's some discussion about whether we're now entering a mass extinction or whether we're already in one, and if it's the sixth mass extinction, the seventh or eighth. Something we can't argue with is that regardless of what number mass extinction this is or how far into it we might be, the only species to blame is us.

Because our species is causing such an impact on Earth's environments and the species which inhabit them, we've adopted a new name for this time period and this particular mass extinction. It's called the Anthropocene (an-throp O-SEEN) period and the Anthropocene mass extinction.

The name Anthropocene comes from the Ancient Greek words 'anthropos', meaning 'human', and '-cene' which means 'recent' or 'new'. The Anthropocene falls within the timeframe called the Holocene (hol-O SEEN), which started just over 11,500 years ago. Scientists haven't yet completely accepted the Anthropocene, so there's still discussion over exactly when it started. Some believe it should be recorded as having started between 15,000 and 12,000 years ago, when human agriculture started. With the development of farming, habitats changed. Animals that competed with farming were hunted, and livestock animals replaced wild animals in many places.

Others believe the Anthropocene should start around the year 1500, when we see an increase in the rates of extinctions in the historical records of species around the world at a higher rate than the usual level of everyday, 'background' extinctions.

Others still think that the point when the first atomic bomb was dropped in 1945, ending the Second World War, should mark the start of the Anthropocene. As discussions between scientists continue, we should have a better definition of the Anthropocene in the next few years.

CAUSES

We've had asteroids crashing into us at over 70,000km per hour, ocean-choking toxic algae, towering glaciers causing a frozen planet, and lava fields causing a fiery planet. There are differences and there are similarities in the story of life on Earth, but what sets the current Anthropocene apart is that *this* mass extinction has been caused by humans.

When we look at the Anthropocene, it seems to split into two sections. The first section seems to be about specific causes that affected specific species and habitats. Often, we see the same story. We killed stuff. Lots of stuff. And we did it really well. We did it directly through hunting for food, such as the island-living dodo, which

Great auk

disappeared around 1662, or the huge Steller's sea cow, which went extinct in 1768. Some animals were hunted into extinction for sport, such as the Atlas bears, which were used to fight Roman gladiators. Others were hunted for their body parts, such as the great auk, whose feathers were used for pillows, or the sea mink which was hunted for its fur. Other species, like the beautiful, stripy thylacine, were killed off because they were killers themselves, and rather than understand them, we (unnecessarily) feared them. As bad as these extinctions were in the early phase of the Anthropocene, they mostly affected individual species or destroyed limited habitats. We didn't see groups of organisms being driven into extinction or entire ecosystems destroyed.

Sea mink

But we've stopped seeing localised effects and instead started to witness the worldwide effects of this newest mass extinction event. This change is largely because the causes have shifted. Hunting still goes on and individual species are still being driven towards extinction, and local habitats are still being cut down, burned or poisoned, but the causes behind the phase of the Anthropocene we're now in have ramped up and increased.

It all started happening in a period known as the Industrial Revolution. Stretching between 1760 and 1820, across Europe and the USA, this was a time in history when we changed the way we produced practically everything. We went from a handmade approach to using machines, and suddenly, we had steam-power, water-power and, eventually, electricity. Factories popped up everywhere and we developed new chemical processes for production.

Steller's sea cow

Adzebill

Local production turned into global industry. To power these factories, machines and the new processes which went with them, we burned coal, oil and gas. These came out of the ground and are known as *fossil fuels*, because they were produced millions of years ago, and were sometimes literally made up from fossils. Two problems with fossil fuels are that they are in limited supply and their extraction from the ground or seabed causes a lot of localised damage and pollution.

There is a third problem, however, and this is the biggest issue: fossil fuels have a devastating by-product. Lots of reactions have a by-product, such as rubbing your hands together fast creates heat, or the buzz of a bee isn't because it *means* to buzz, but because the noise is made as its wings beat at over 200 times a second. When fossil fuels are burned as part of the process to create energy, they release greenhouse gases as a by-product, and it's these greenhouse gases that cause massive damage around the world. Like an actual greenhouse, greenhouse gases trap heat. They prevent the trapped heat from escaping through our atmosphere.

There are lots of different greenhouse gases, but you might be familiar with carbon dioxide, or CO_2. Although we need some carbon dioxide in order to keep the planet warm, more and more carbon dioxide means more and more heat is trapped. Too much carbon dioxide means too much heat is trapped, eventually causing global warming, which is a major environmental problem. The planet overheats, making it harder for species to survive.

Scientists today are constantly worried about the levels of carbon dioxide being released into the atmosphere and it's important we measure and monitor the volume to gauge changes. At the moment, we estimate that around 40 gigatonnes of carbon dioxide is released into our atmosphere every year. It's hard to imagine how much this really is, but a single gigatonne

Goliath Tenerife lizard

is the same as one trillion kilograms, about the weight of a trillion bags of sugar!

Although you might not think it, the Earth's average temperature now is around 15°C, but throughout the Earth's history, it has been much, much warmer. At the end of the Permian period, for example, our planet baked in heatwaves of 60°C, while coastal marine habitats may have been as high as 40°C. If this sounds familiar, then you may remember that these massive changes in greenhouse gases and the devastating climate change they caused were responsible for the worst mass extinction the Earth has ever seen. If that sounds worrying, then that's probably not a bad thing, as we should be worried that history (or prehistory) doesn't repeat itself now.

Climate change is the biggest issue in terms of habitat destruction, biodiversity loss and ultimately extinction, but it's not the only problem. We have almost as many causes in this current extinction crisis as

Atlas bear

we have species threatened with extinction.

Koala lemur

Habitat destruction is also brought about by more direct actions. Across the planet, marine habitats are being destroyed intentionally. Around the UK for example, a whopping 97 per cent of British marine protected areas are dredged, to collect stones and shingle for the building industry, or are bottom-trawled, to catch fish and other marine species. Terrestrial habitats are being cut down, burned, mined, poisoned and eroded.

Human-instigated habitat destruction has reduced the number of trees on our planet by almost 50 per cent since human civilisation emerged. This is also seen in more specific habitats such as tropical forests, which have been slashed (quite literally) from approximately 16 million square kilometres to less than nine million square kilometres today. Scientists estimate that approximately 15 billion trees are cut down each year. You might need to read that again and really think about that number.

Habitats everywhere are being destroyed: forests are cut down, grasslands burned, coastal habitats ruined. A turtle desperately tries to avoid being trapped in a huge dredging net, which catches any species living in or close to the sand bed. This type of fishing destroys coral reefs, seagrass beds and fish nurseries. The damage can last for hundreds of years.

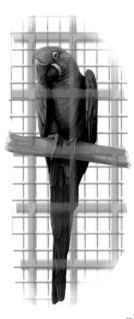

It's shocking. Only 15 per cent of the land area of Europe remains unchanged by humans.

Across the globe, approximately 20 per cent of marine coastal areas have been highly modified by our actions. Thirty-five per cent of mangrove habitats have been destroyed. About 20 per cent of coral reefs have been destroyed, and a further 20 per cent have been severely degraded by overfishing, pollution and invasive species. In some places, over 90 per cent of coral reef systems have been destroyed.

Hunting causes problems for many species. Elephants are killed for their tusks, rhinos for their horns, pangolins for their scales, sharks for their fins, bears for their bile, and countless other species for various reasons.

Similarly, the illegal pet trade in wild animals is devastating populations and driving many more species towards extinction. Marine fish from coral reefs, birds, reptiles, invertebrates such as tarantulas and scorpions, and many mammals, including monkeys and their relatives, are all illegally taken from the wild, kept in poor conditions and often die within their first year of being a pet. With the added threat of pollution, from plastics to toxic chemicals, many more animals are entangled in rubbish, poisoned or have the ability to breed and produce offspring removed.

It's clear that there is an avalanche of causes behind the current extinction crisis. Climate change is the most significant, but we would be very silly to ignore the habitat destruction, the hunting and killing, the exploitation, the pollution and every other threat facing life on our planet. If we don't tackle *all* of the problems, then we're still left with a problem.

Millions of people rely on food from the sea to survive. But fishing practices vary. The use of longline fishing leads to the accidental capture (or 'bycatch') of dolphins, turtles and birds, like this albatross. We have to think about where our food comes from and our impact on our planet.

EFFECTS

Since climate change is the greatest threat to face the planet right now, including our own species, we need to better understand it and exactly what happens when extra carbon dioxide is pumped into our atmosphere.

Although there's a pretty long list of impacts, the two most relevant and devastating in terms of mass extinctions are first, global warming, which affects everything from which plants can grow in an area to when different species can breed, and second, increasing carbon dioxide levels, which cause a major issue in the oceans and marine ecosystems around the world.

Carbon dioxide is absorbed by seawater, and the more there is, the more is absorbed. When these two ingredients react, they form an acid, called carbonic acid, which over time will increase the acidity of the seawater itself. When this happens, it can damage huge parts of a marine ecosystem by killing small organisms that have either soft external skeletons or shells that are destroyed by the acid.

Scientists have shown that our oceans have increased in acidity by 25 per cent in the last two hundred years or so. Looking ahead, and unless we take drastic action, this level will increase, making it difficult for marine species to survive.

As scientists, we can't just talk about 'too much' or 'too little' of something, without knowing what the ideal levels are; we need to go a step further. So, how much carbon dioxide should be in the atmosphere? We calculate this by looking at the ratio of a particular gas in relation to another and we use a unit called 'parts per million' (or ppm). If, for example, we look at the amount of krypton found in air (which is one of the many gases that make up our atmosphere), we'd see that it represents a little bit over 1ppm. This means that the other 999,999 molecules within our sample of atmosphere are from gases other than Krypton. If we look at the carbon dioxide in our atmosphere right now, it's around 412ppm. When we look back over the last two hundred years, since the start of the Industrial Revolution, we see this has increased by a worrying 50 per cent in that time. The rate of carbon dioxide currently being released is the fastest since before the End Permian mass extinction. This means we are well on our way to burning through all the available fossil fuels on and in our planet, where we might release as much as an extra 5,000 gigatonnes of carbon dioxide into our atmosphere.

Climate change does have devastating effects for biodiversity; some take their time, others have rapid results. In 2020, exceptionally dry conditions led to terrible bushfires which raged for months across large parts of the world. Although we'll never know for sure, scientists have estimated that billions of animals were killed, with 143 million mammals, 2.46 billion reptiles, 180 million birds and 51 million frogs killed or being forced to move.

Elsewhere, polar bears are losing the ice cover they need to hunt, walruses are losing feeding grounds and tens of thousands of reindeer are dying in some winters as a result of climate change.

We have some marine invertebrates that are literally dissolving because the oceans are becoming more acidic. Marine turtle eggs are being affected, creating problems with the number of males and females which hatch, and some species of whales are having to travel further to feed, as warmer waters are affecting the distribution of the plankton many of them need to survive. The truth is that there are hundreds (and probably thousands) of examples of how species are threatened by climate change right now. The important thing is not to become upset by this bad news, but to be determined to do something about it.

Fossil fuels affect our planet on a wide scale, influencing our climate and, at a local level, polluting our environments. This oil spill has coated the feathers of some unfortunate seabirds. Unless the oil can be removed, the birds cannot dive, hunt for food or clean themselves and they will die.

Wahaj Mahmood-Brown is a marine biologist, studying for his PhD on the restoration of seagrass meadows. He is a member of the Marine Biological Association and specialises in ecology – how communities of living things interact with the environment. He works at the British Phycological Society, raising awareness of the importance of seaweed for wildlife, the environment and people.

Why are marine environments so important?

Did you know that we are living in an ice age? The North and South poles are still cloaked in ice from the cold Pleistocene era that ended 10,000 years ago, when woolly mammoths roamed the Earth. In the Holocene era that followed, the climate became milder and more stable. Weather became more predictable and reliable seasonal rain led to humans developing farming, allowing us to dominate the planet and the rise of civilisations.

For the last 10,000 years, we have enjoyed the longest period of stable mild weather in the Earth's 4.5 billion year history, thanks to the ocean. The way in which currents of water move in the ocean creates the Goldilocks effect for Earth's climate: not too hot and not too cold. This is helped by the white of the ice sheets at the poles, which reflect the energy from sunlight back into space.

The ocean covers most of the Earth's surface, and every other breath we take comes from oxygen produced by phytoplankton. But marine wildlife is not found in the same numbers everywhere. The shallow seas around our coasts are the most productive, both for wildlife and people. These include coral reefs, seagrass meadows and kelp forests. People have been fishing and living by the coast for thousands of years. But since the Industrial Revolution began in the 18th century, our population has increased tenfold. With industrialised fishing, coastal urbanisation and pollution, marine wildlife is under extreme pressure.

The biggest threat of all is climate change because of our use of fossil fuels and the build-up of carbon dioxide (CO_2) in our atmosphere, which reduces the amount of excess heat on Earth escaping into space. The ocean has absorbed most of this CO_2, but not without a price. CO_2 makes seawater more acidic, so many animals like corals, sea snails and phytoplankton find it harder to build their hard, chalky body parts. The International Union for Conservation of Nature suggests that these pressures may cause the extinction of a third of all marine species.

One of the most important types of marine habitats are seagrass meadows. Seagrasses are the only plants that have evolved to live submerged in the ocean and are found in shallow waters all over the world. They are nurseries for young fish and create habitats for hundreds of other species including sea turtles, manatees and seahorses. Amazingly, they lock away more CO_2 than tropical rainforests.

But in the UK, 90 per cent of seagrass meadows have been lost. Because of this, charities like the Ocean Conservation Trust are replanting seagrass meadows, with the aim of reducing carbon dioxide in the atmosphere and restoring the biodiversity in our coastal waters. To help their efforts, I am developing techniques during my PhD to clone seagrasses in the laboratory, so that together, we can plant them in the meadows even faster. So next time you are at a sandy beach at low tide, keep an eye out for the humble yet mighty seagrass. It's vital to our survival.

CONSERVATION

I'M HOPING that when you read this, you've read the rest of my series and you've enjoyed getting this far. I also hope that you have a much better understanding of the process of extinction and the role it plays within an ecosystem and how mass extinctions have shaped our world. My final hope is that now you know the threats facing our planet and the species living on it, you'll want to do something to help.

The good news is that you can. Not only is this the first mass extinction ever where one species is responsible for the extinction of so many others, but it's also the first where one species is actively trying to save others. We call this conservation.

Demonic poison frog

If you ask 10 different people what they think conservation is about, you'll probably get 10 different answers. A lot of people seem to have the idea that conservation is about cuddling cute orphan animals and that you spend your days playing with baby tigers, pandas and orangutans. If you're thinking that, then please, think again.

If we look for a simple definition of conservation, then it's the actions aimed at saving species, habitats and ecosystems. Conservation is a highly important area of science, backed up and supported by lots of strong (and often complex) research. Conservationists are not 'animal cuddlers', they are biologists, botanists, veterinarians, mathematicians, economists, geologists, physicists, chemists and a host of other people from science, banking, business, education and other fields of expertise. To make something like conservation work you don't only need people who know about plants and animals, you need experts from different backgrounds.

If you were on one of the courses I teach, I'd spend time talking about how species evolve and how best we can save them. There's a lot to learn, but something I teach early on is that being a conservationist is less about the animals or plants you're trying to save and more about working alongside people, whether local communities, companies, businesses or governments. There will always be people who say that the animals being saved are more important than the local people involved. Those people are idiots and the truth is they don't make good conservationists at all.

Do a little experiment for me and think of three different species that are both threatened with extinction and which, in your mind, definitely need to be saved. OK, done that? Now, I've not had professional training as a mind reader but I'm guessing your list doesn't include anything like a slug, frog or vulture. I'm 100 per cent assuming plants weren't even an inkling in your head (and yes, I did say 'species' and not 'species of *animals*'). I'd be willing to bet money that your list included animals such as tigers, polar bears and, of course, many people's favourite, the panda. Am I right?

Kakapo

There appear to be *favourites* among those species considered most 'worthy' of conservation support and usually, most of us think of animals before plants. I'm guessing your list of animals didn't include the humble European eel, the bizarre kakapo from New Zealand or the tragic vaquita from Mexico. They are all critically endangered and represent a fish, bird and mammal that arguably need more help than the beautiful tiger, the stunning polar bear and the cute panda. So why do some species get more help when others are clearly in as much, if not more, need? It seems unfair. Well, it makes more sense when you think of conservation like a business. The truth is that we do not have the money or energy to support every single species that needs our help.

Think about it: if you want to save some incredibly rare species of snail in a forest, do you think you're going to get a lot of support? I'll tell you now you will have a hard time raising money. And, if you do raise enough money, it

Vaquita

will be unlikely that you will
be able to save anything other than the
snails and maybe the plants they feed on. Now, imagine
there are also some monkeys in the same forest. Cute and
cuddly, their faces are simply adorable. I don't actually
think that about monkeys, but you can see how they might
be more popular than the rare snails. The monkeys are an
instant win and it's easy to imagine how much more easily
the money will roll in. Even if the monkeys don't need as
much help, there's an argument that focusing on them may
be a better tactic. Not only would you probably be more
successful in raising money but also by using the monkeys
as a focus, you would indirectly be able to save
lots of other animals, plants and other
organisms within the forest. It's all
about what we call *flagship* species
and *umbrella* species.

European eel

Conservation of the bigger, more popular and sometimes cuter species can help others that are less well known. By protecting chimpanzees in the forests of Uganda, I was also able to help the rhinoceros viper, giant pangolin, birds such as the small brown Puvel's illadopsis, the giant African swallowtail butterfly and even trees such as the mahogany.

A flagship species gets its name direct from history. In the olden days, if two countries decided to go to war and both had navies, it was important to know exactly who was on whose side. So both sides would have a flagship, which was exactly what it sounds like – a ship with a great big flag attached to it. The flagship sailed at the front of the fleet letting everyone know who the ships belonged to, avoiding that awkward situation where either you fired canons at your mates, or invited a bunch of pirates over. A flagship species acts in much the same way. It is chosen because it can be used to represent lots of other species. A way to look at flagship species is to see them as something similar to being conservation mascots. They represent something bigger, and helping them can help others too.

Then there are the umbrella species. This is a similar idea, in which one species benefits many others, but whereas the flagship species is often intentionally selected, an umbrella species can be accidental. Flagships can be used to help other species in terms of financial support, but protecting an umbrella species has a more immediate impact on other species. Whereas a flagship can be used to help unrelated and unconnected species anywhere in the world, umbrella species help other species living within the same habitat or ecosystem. There are plenty of other conservation tools that are used in various ways, but flagship and umbrella species are used throughout conservation.

Another very important part of conservation is to work with local people in what we call community development programmes. This is a huge, broad area of conservation and we could easily discuss it for hours. Very loosely, it can be divided into two main areas: helping local communities get what they physically want, such as building wells or clinics or buying farmland, and helping them obtain things that are maybe less material, but arguably more important, such as better health care and education. By working with local communities, it's easier to protect local species, habitats and ecosystems.

We are causing problems, but we can be vital in saving species, habitats and ecosystems too. The more we learn about our planet, the more we understand it. Communities and individuals are replanting and regenerating habitats and caring for species, while entire countries are protecting environments.

WHAT CAN YOU DO?

Imagine your favourite species for a few moments. Maybe it's a chimpanzee or a clown fish, a raven, an olm or a skink, or an oak tree or a Venus flytrap. Now imagine a world without your favourite species. They're gone. Extinct. It's a sad prospect, isn't it? How will we explain to our children or grandchildren what happened if we allow these amazing species to be pushed into extinction, existing only in history books? So much work is being done all around the world, by governments, schools and universities, companies, community groups and, very importantly, by individuals, showing that there is something each of us can do, regardless of how small we are, or how quiet we think our voice is.

Anemone fish

We have to remain positive and optimistic, and believe that each of us is capable of making a difference. If we don't, then what's the point in trying? You might think my series is about extinction, but really, it's been preparing you for this. It's been giving you the knowledge you need to move forward.

Olm

It all comes down to this next short sentence.

YOU HAVE THE POWER TO CHANGE THE WORLD.

That's it. It might sound simple, or it might sound impossible, but it's true and I need you to believe it.

How and where we shop makes a big difference. When we shop locally and buy seasonal, local foods, it reduces the energy spent on growing things out of season, or transporting them thousands of kilometres around the world.

I'm a vegetarian but it's not always possible to completely change your diet. Maybe get your family to reduce the amount of meat they eat, or see whether your school will do a meat-free Monday. If you want to go further and change your diet, that's up to you, but eating sustainably caught fish, or local, organic meat is better than no change at all.

Barred owl

Venus flytrap

Look out for a product called palm oil on labels when you buy things from the supermarket and do a bit of research to see why it's such an amazing oil, but why it is causing so many habitat problems in Asia and now Africa, and why it is driving the three orangutan species into extinction. Hopefully, we'll see more labels saying 'sustainable palm oil' in the years ahead.

Recycle whenever possible, reduce the amount of packaging waste you throw away, and definitely cut the amount of single-use plastic you buy and use, as much as you can. Little things such as using a canvas bag for shopping, reusable cups for tea and coffee and not taking plastic drinking straws really help.

Plant some wildflowers, leave a patch of your garden to grow wild and use your bike or walk more.

Pick up some litter, or get your school to organise a clean-up event in your local park. Maybe join a beach clean.

Every action helps, and the world will thank you for it. A lot of people will say you can't make a difference or that these things won't change the world but they're wrong. Maybe they're being lazy, maybe they don't care, or maybe they have a reason to make people feel they can't change the world. It doesn't matter. *You* have the power to sway companies, influence governments and change the world. Don't forget that and never ever let anyone tell you otherwise.

And while I can only hope you might one day become a scientist (because it is the best job in the world, obviously), I know it might not suit everyone. So, whether you become a scientist or not, I want you to think like a scientist. Follow the evidence. Look at the data. Don't believe something just because you want to believe it, or because the person telling you is popular, or famous, or just the loudest person in the room. Weigh up the evidence, even if it's not the answer you want. If more of us think like this and follow the science, the world will be a much better place.

So, what does the future for life on Earth look like? I don't know. None of us do. What I am certain of is that the natural world is under greater threat now than at any other time in human history. The next few years will be pivotal and the future of life on Earth is in our hands. And if it worries you that so many habitats are being destroyed and so many species are threatened with extinction, then remember that never before in the whole history of life on our planet have these habitats and species had so many people fighting for their survival. And you're one of them.

GLOSSARY

Biodiversity (BI-O DIE-vers it-EE)
The variety of plants, fungi, animals and other groups of organisms within a particular habitat or ecosystem. A healthy habitat or ecosystem will usually have higher levels of biodiversity.

Carbon dioxide
A naturally occurring greenhouse gas. At normal levels, carbon dioxide is essential for trapping some levels of heat energy within our environment. When levels get too high, overheating occurs.

Ecology
The particular area of biology in which the focus is on the relationship between organisms and their physical surroundings.

Environment (en-vire-on ment)
The 'surroundings' in which an organism, or group of organisms, lives. This includes other species but also weather, climate, mountains, deserts, rivers, lakes, oceans and so on.

Fauna (for-naa)
The animals found in a particular place or from a particular time.

Flagship species
In conservation, a flagship species acts as a mascot or representative, to help represent other species or habitats.

Gigatonne
A way to measure the force of an explosion. One gigatonne is the same as one trillion kilograms, about the weight of a trillion bags of sugar or the same force as one billion sticks of dynamite exploding at the same time.

Greenhouse gas
Like an actual greenhouse, greenhouse gases are able to trap heat. They prevent the trapped heat from

escaping through our atmosphere. Carbon dioxide is a greenhouse gas. We need greenhouse gases to keep our planet warm enough for life to exist, but if their levels get too high, we start seeing environmental problems through global warming.

Organism (or-gan IZ-mm)
Any living thing. A tree is an organism, so is a shark, and a mushroom. You are an organism.

Primate
Any member of the group that contains apes, monkeys, lemurs, bush babies and lorises. These mammals are social, have large brains, nails on their fingers and toes, and other physical characteristics which help link them.

Umbrella species
Any species used in conservation to help represent or protect other species within the same habitat or environment.

Zoonotic (ZOO not-ik) **disease**
Any disease which starts in animals then jumps to humans, infecting us.

Collect all eight titles
in the EXTINCT series

 *Hallucigenia*

 *Dunkleosteus*

 Trilobite

Lisowicia

 *Tyrannosaurus rex*

 *Megalodon*

Thylacine

 *Hainan gibbon*

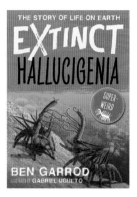

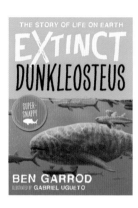

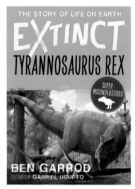

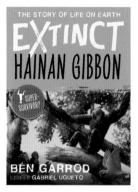

Collect all eight titles in the EXTINCT series

THE STORY OF LIFE ON EARTH

EXTINCT
HALLUCIGENIA

SUPER-WEIRD

BEN GARROD
ILLUSTRATED BY GABRIEL UGUETO

One of the oldest and most mysterious animals ever described, *Hallucigenia* was a kind of sea-living, armoured worm. But it was nothing like the worms we know today. Its body was covered in spines and frills. It had claws at the end of its legs and a mouth lined with sharp teeth.

This strange animal was one of the victims of the End Ordovician mass extinction which claimed 85 per cent of the species living in the world's oceans around 443 million years ago. What could have led to this catastrophe and what caused the appearance of huge glaciers and falling sea levels, leaving many marine ecosystems dry and unable to sustain life at a time when it had only just got started?

An armoured fish with a bite 10 times more powerful than that of a great white shark, *Dunkleosteus* could also snap its jaws five times faster than you can blink! It was one of the most iconic predators ever to rule the waves. What was it like to live in its shadow? And how did it become one of the many victims of the Late Devonian mass extinction around 375 million years ago?

Let's discover why this mass extinction only affected ocean life and why it went on for so long – some scientists believe it lasted for 25 million years. In a weird twist, we'll look at whether the evolution of trees on the land at that time was partly responsible for the loss of so many marine species, including *Dunkleosteus*.

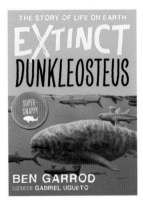

THE STORY OF LIFE ON EARTH

EXTINCT
DUNKLEOSTEUS

SUPER-SNAPPY

BEN GARROD
ILLUSTRATED BY GABRIEL UGUETO

Among the first arthropods – animals with jointed legs such as insects and their relatives – trilobites were around on Earth for over 300 million years and survived the first two mass extinctions. There were once at least 20,000 species but all disappeared in the devastating End Permian mass extinction around 252 million years ago.

We'll look at why land animals were affected this time as well as those in the sea. An incredible 96 per cent of marine species went extinct and an almost equally terrible 70 per cent of life on land was wiped out in what is known as the *Great Dying*. This was the closest we've come to losing all life on Earth and the planet was changed forever.

At a massive 9 tonnes, the elephant-sized *Lisowicia* was one of the largest animals on the planet during the Late Triassic. A kind of cross between a mammal and a reptile but not quite either, *Lisowicia* was a distant cousin of the ancient mammals – and they eventually led to our very own ancestors.

We'll discover why the End Triassic mass extinction happened, changing the global environment and making life impossible for around 75 per cent of species. And how, while this fourth mass extinction may have been devastating for most life on Earth, it gave one group of animals – dinosaurs – the chance to dominate the planet for millions of years.

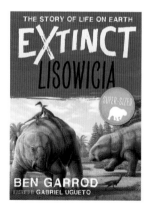

Weighing as much as three adult elephants and as long as a bus, *Tyrannosaurus rex* was one of the mightiest land predators that has ever lived. It had the most powerful bite of any dinosaur and dominated its environment. But not even the biggest dinosaurs were a match for what happened at the end of the Cretaceous, about 66 million years ago.

What happened when an asteroid travelling at almost 40,000km/h crashed into Earth? Creating a shockwave that literally shook the world, its impact threw millions of tonnes of red-hot ash and dust into the atmosphere, blocking out the sun and destroying 75 per cent of life on Earth. Any living thing bigger than a fox was gone and this fifth global mass extinction meant the end of the dinosaurs as we knew them.

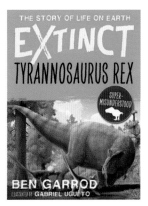

A giant marine predator, megalodon grew up to an incredible 18m – longer than three great white sharks, nose to tail. This ferocious monster had the most powerful bite force ever measured. It specialised in killing whales by attacking them from the side, aiming for their heart and lungs.

But, like more than 50 per cent of marine mammals and many other creatures, megalodon disappeared in the End Pliocene mass extinction around 2.5 million years ago. We'll find out why this event affected many of the bigger animals in the marine environment and had an especially bad impact on both warm-blooded animals and predators.

The thylacine, also known as the Tasmanian tiger, is one of a long list of species, ranging from sabre-toothed cats to the dodo, that have been wiped out by humans. The last wild thylacine was shot in 1930 and the last captive thylacine alive died in a zoo in 1936.

We'll explore the mass extinction we are now entering and how we, as a species, have the power to wipe out other species – something no other single species is able to do. Who are the winners and losers and why might it take over seven million years to restore mammal diversity on Earth to what it was before humans arrived?

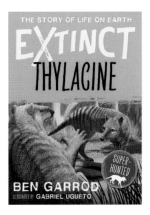

BEN GARROD is Professor of Evolutionary Biology and Science Engagement at the University of East Anglia. Ben has lived and worked all around the world, alongside chimpanzees in Africa, polar bears in the Arctic and giant dinosaur fossils in South America. He is currently based in the West Country. He broadcasts regularly on TV and radio and is a trustee and ambassador of a number of key conservation organisations. His eight book series *Ultimate Dinosaurs* and *The Chimpanzee and Me* are also published by Zephyr.

GABRIEL UGUETO is a scientific illustrator, palaeoartist and herpetologist based in Florida. For several years, he was an independent herpetologist researcher and authored papers on new species of neotropical lizards and various taxonomic revisions. As an illustrator, his work reflects the latest scientific hypotheses about the external appearance and the behaviour of the animals, both extinct and extant, that he reconstructs. His illustrations have appeared in books, journals, magazines, museum exhibitions and television documentaries.

Zephyr is an imprint of Head of Zeus.
At Zephyr we are proud to publish books
you can read and re-read time and time
again because they tell a brilliant story
and because they entertain you.

 @_ZephyrBooks

 @_zephyrbooks

 HeadofZeusBooks

readzephyr.com

www.headofzeus.com

ZEPHYR